Programmer's Guide to the EGA and VGA Cards

Second Edition